Licensed by:

Hasbro

DREAMWORKS PICTURES

Paramount
A VIACOM COMPANY

GM
OFFICIAL
LICENSED PRODUCT

General Motors trademarks used under license to Hasbro, Inc.

BENDON

Bendon Publishing International, Inc.
Ashland, OH 44805
www.bendonpub.com

BUMBLEBEE:

CRACK the CODE!

Using the Transformers' alphabet below,
fill in the blanks and reveal the secret words!

___ ___ ___ ___ ___ ___ ___

___ ___   ___ ___ ___

___ ___ ___ ___ ___ ___

A	B	C	D	E	F	G	H	I

J	K	L	M	N	O	P	Q	R

S	T	U	V	W	X	Y	Z

WHICH IS DIFFERENT?

One Autobot below is an imposter. Can you find the
one that is different from the others?

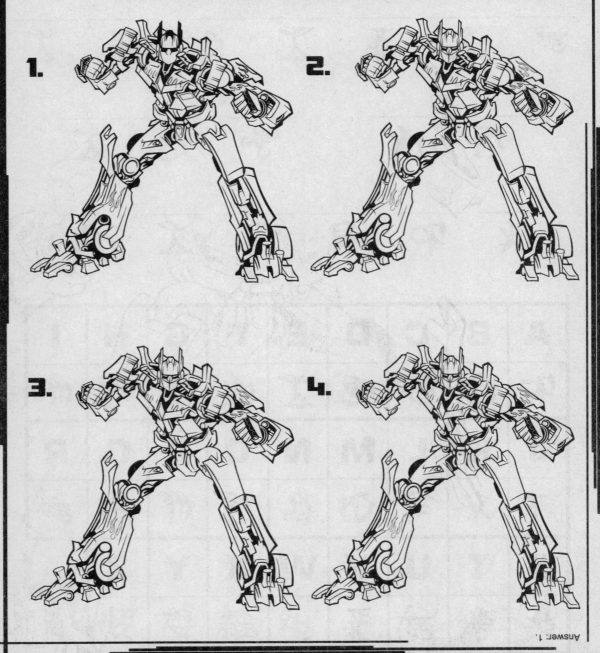

1.

2.

3.

4.

Finish the Picture!

Using the example below as a guide,
complete the picture of Bumblebee.

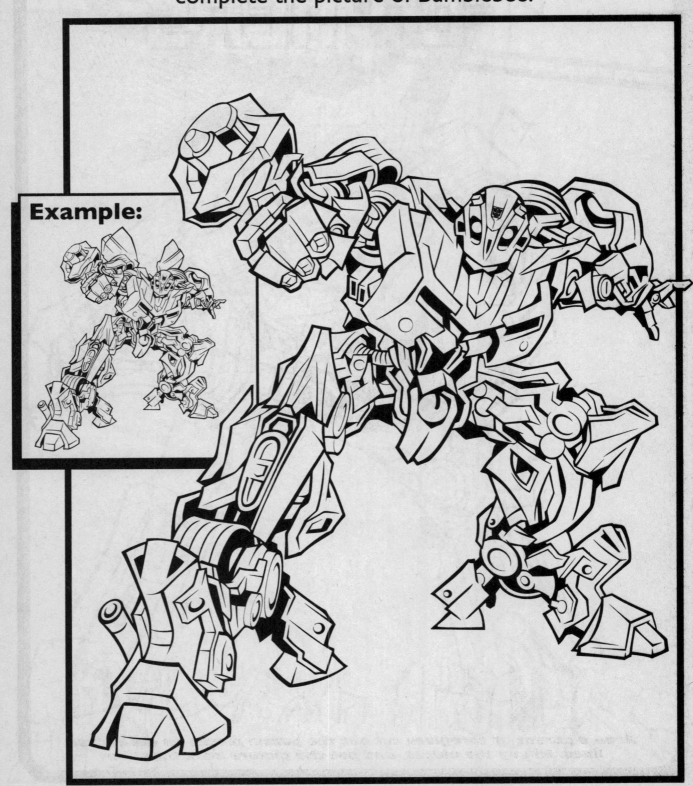

Example:

TRANSFORMERS

REVENGE OF THE FALLEN

PUZZLE

Have a parent or caregiver cut out the puzzle pieces on the dotted lines. Mix up the pieces, and put the picture back together!

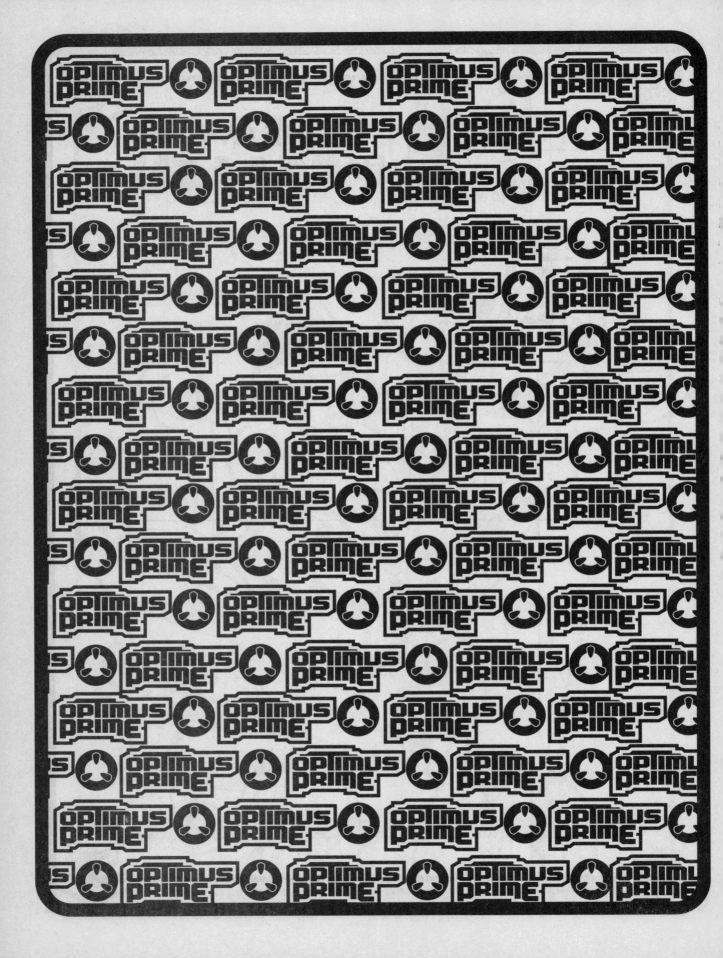

DRAW
THE FALLEN

Using the grid as a guide, draw a picture of **THE FALLEN** in the box below.

HOW MANY WORDS
can you make out of
DEVASTATOR

Follow the Path

Using the letters in order from the word

OPTIMUS PRIME

follow the correct path to find your way through the maze!

START ▼

```
K   S   O   P   T   O   F   D
E   L   J   R   I   R   C   I
N   G   P   G   M   U   S   P
V   R   U   H   L   W   C   R
T   B   T   P   O   E   M   I
X   M   I   W   F   D   B   E
G   U   R   G   Z   I   O   E
O   S   P   R   I   M   E   J
```

FINISH

Make a Match!

Only 2 characters below are exactly the same.
Can you find them?

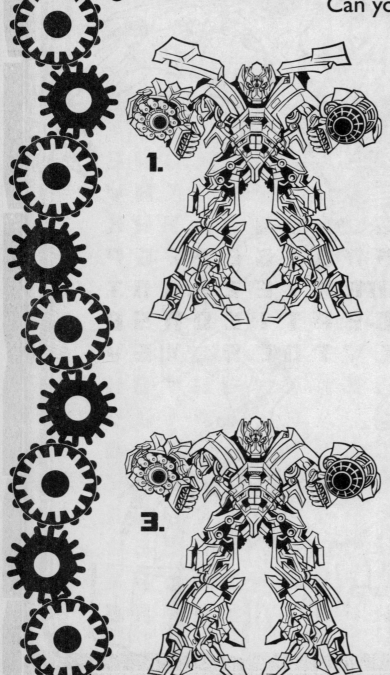

1.

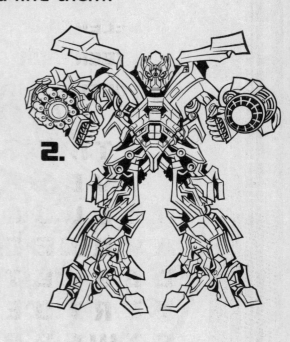

2.

3.

4.

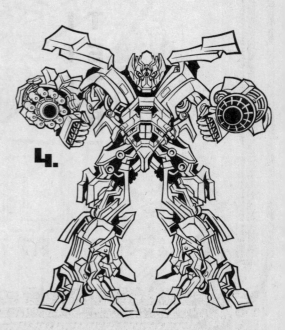

WORD SEARCH

Find and circle the words in the puzzle below.

- ○ **DECEPTICONS**
- ○ **CYBERTRON**
- ○ **FORCE**
- ○ **BATTLE**
- ○ **REVENGE**
- ○ **CONVERT**

```
S J T M U T P U I Y O N K G P B
T Y V B X Z F H X E H G R T H V
N B L U D K S C B L N F A T R K
A V Q W E C F R Q R G O D F G P
C E R K L T M R N J E Z P O N T
Y E R T D E C E P T I C O N S B
B T W E R O C V T Q C O L X E V
E X T L F R Z E R L U N U J O G
R Q E N B K R N O R E V A I B S
T O T G N H F G S L J E V C L O
R P B A T T L E R U S R F H A Z
O P S X E W C V Q P I T T N S K
N X R X T M J S H E F O R C E J
J I E G U V H Y O I H I U G R K
O R D I M I R F O T N K G P R O
```

Word Scramble

Using the words from the list below, unscramble the letters to correctly spell the names and words!

heT llFnea _____

getanorM _____

Oimtpsu emiPr _____

vRaaeg _____

norledih _____

tSrarscmae _____

dMupfla _____

disSk _____

Rtahcte _____

Word List

- The Fallen
- Megatron
- Optimus Prime
- Ratchet
- Skids
- Mudflap
- Ravage
- Ironhide
- Starscream

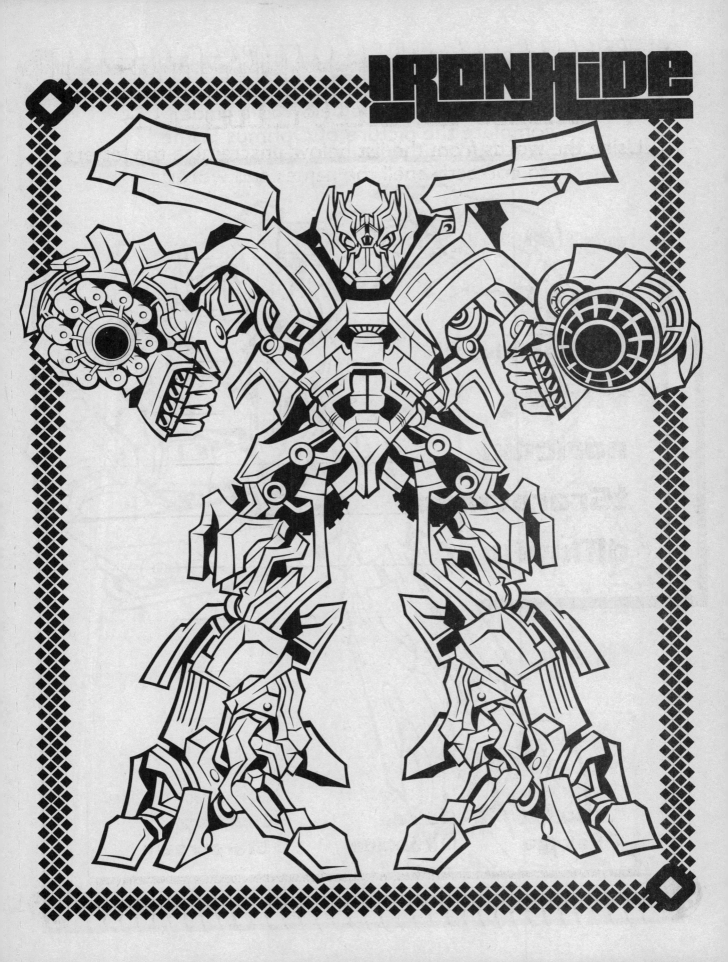

IRONHIDE

Finish the Picture!

Using the example below as a guide,
complete the picture of Optimus Prime.

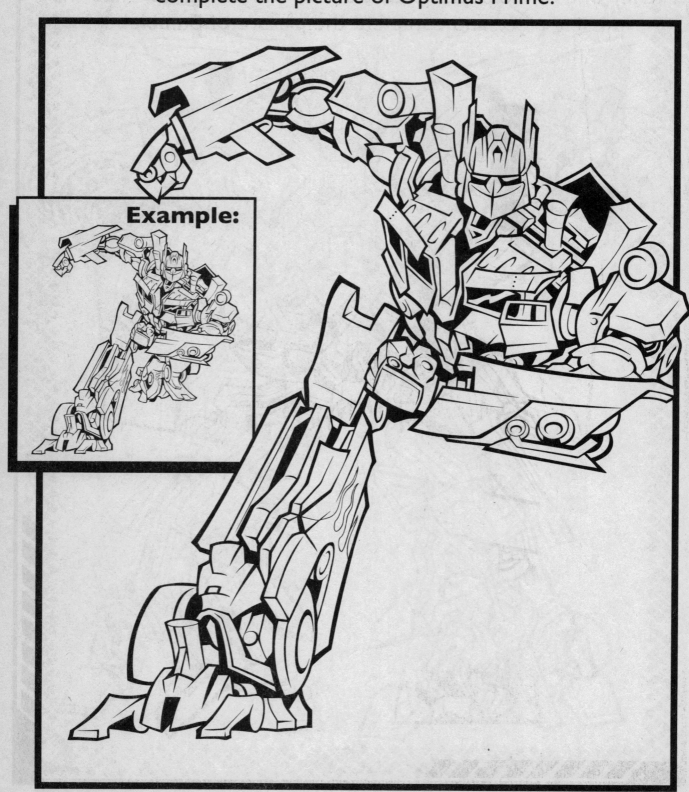

Example:

WHICH PIECE IS MISSING?

Only one of the puzzle pieces below will fit. Can you find the missing piece and complete the picture of Bumblebee?

1.

2.

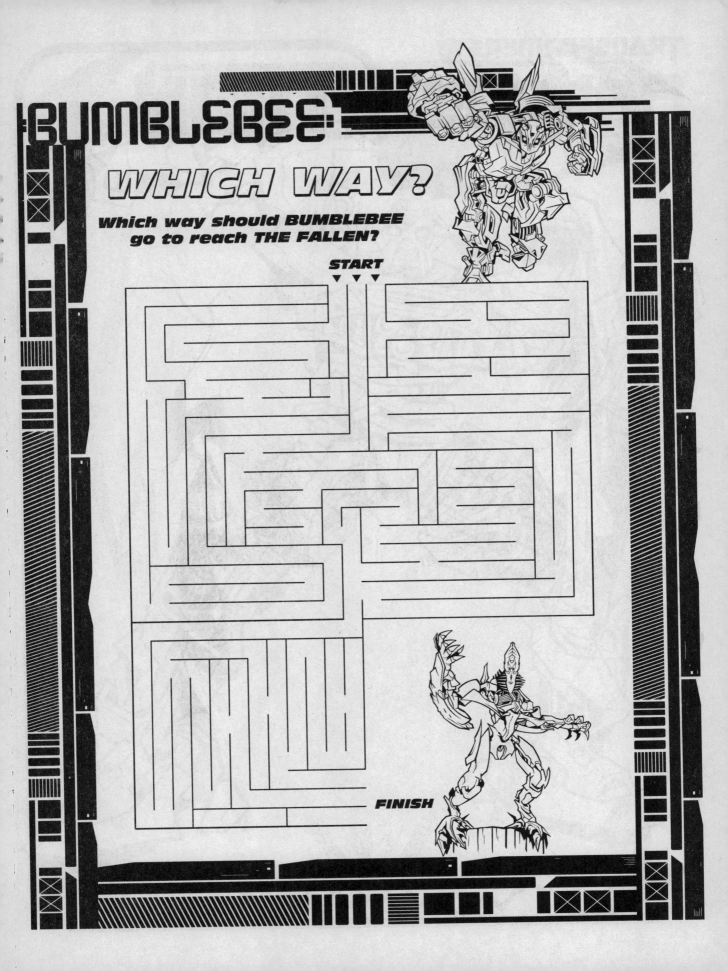

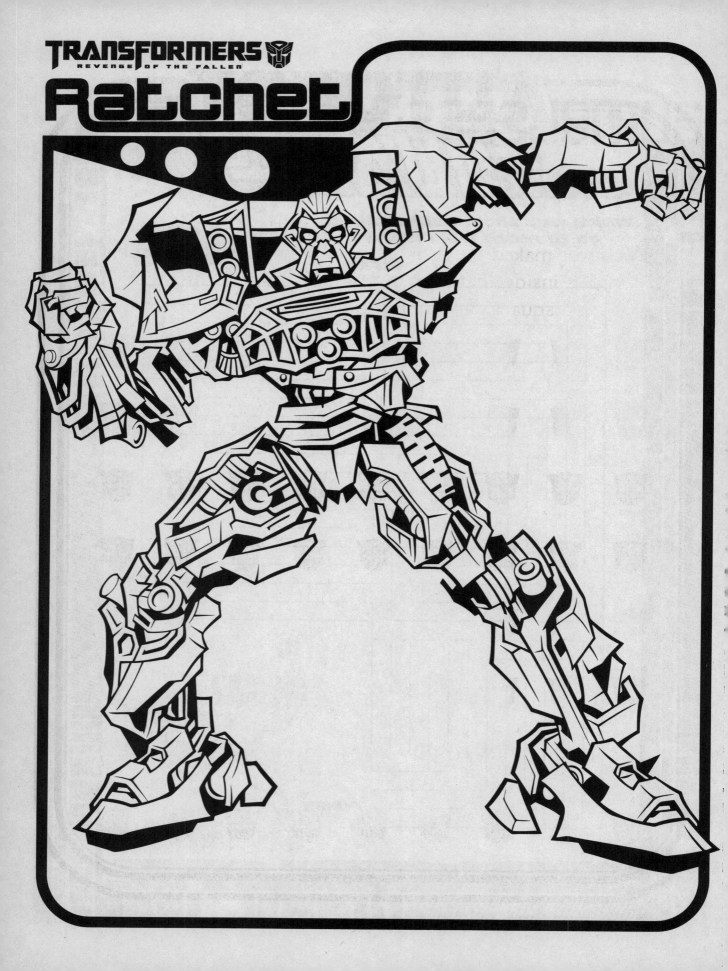

AUTOBOT SQUARES

Taking turns, connect a line from one  to another. Whoever makes the line that completes a box puts their initials inside that square. The person with the most squares at the end of the game wins!

Cross out the word **MEGATRON** every time you see it in the box. When you reach a letter that does not belong, write it in the circles below to reveal the secret message.

MEGATRONRMEGATRONE
MEGATRONVMEGTRONE
MEGATRONNMEGATRONG
MEGATRONEMEGATRONO
MEGATRONFMEGATRON
TMEGATRONMEGATRONH
MEGATRONEMEGATRONF
MEGATRONAMEGATRONL
MEGATRONLMEGATRONE
MEGATRONMEGATRONN

◯ ◯ ◯ ◯ ◯ ◯ ◯ ◯ ◯

◯ ◯ ◯ ◯ ◯ ◯ ◯ ◯ ◯ ◯ ◯

DRAW
STAR
SCREAM

Using the grid as a guide,
draw a picture of
STARSCREAM
in the box below.

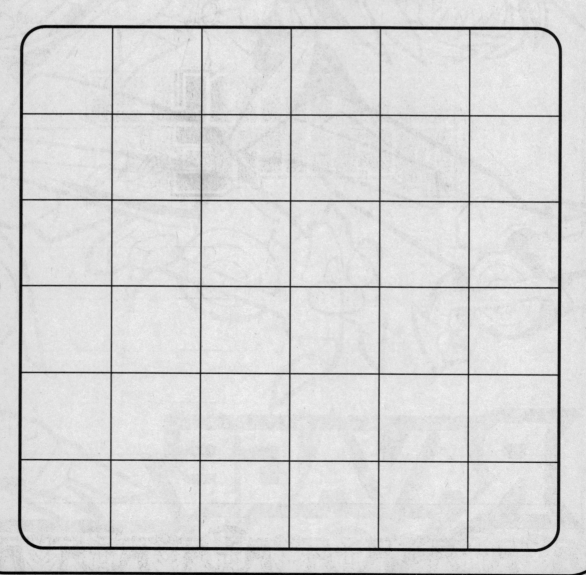

HOW MANY WORDS

can you make out of the word

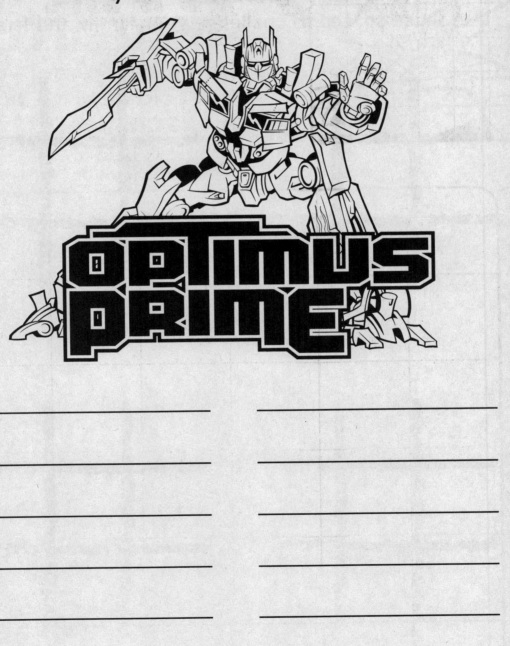

_____   _____

_____   _____

_____   _____

_____   _____

_____   _____

_____   _____

TIC-TAC-TOE

Use these spaces to challenge your family and friends.

Follow the Path

Using the letters in order from the word
BUMBLEBEE
follow the correct path to find your way through the maze!

START

K	R	B	N	T	K	S	G
E	M	U	S	B	U	M	F
K	B	T	E	E	U	B	M
V	L	E	B	L	E	L	G
T	B	T	P	E	B	M	I
C	M	U	B	E	D	L	E
G	B	R	G	Z	I	O	P
P	L	E	B	E	E	S	J

FINISH

WHICH IS WHICH?

Match each Transformer to its correct shadow.

1.

2.

3.

Answer: 1.B, 2.C, 3.A

Which Piece is
MISSING?

Only one of the puzzle pieces below will fit. Can you find
the missing piece and complete the puzzle?

A.

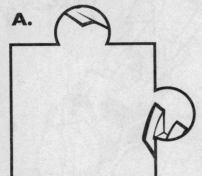

B.

C.

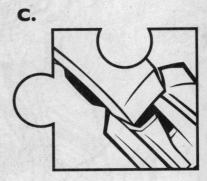

WHICH MUDFLAP IS

DIFFERENT?

One MUDFLAP below is an imposter.
Can you find the one that is different from the others?

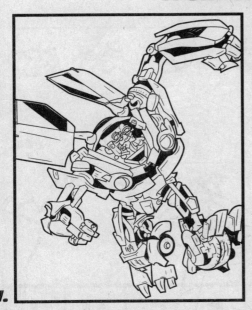

1.

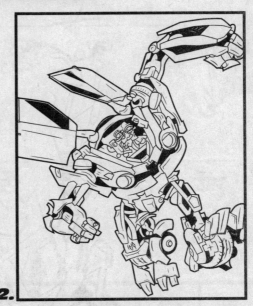

2.

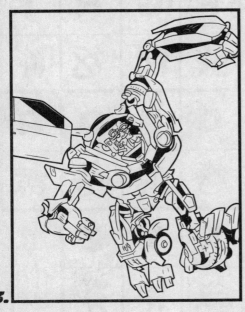

3.

4.

CRACK the CODE!

Using the Transformer's alphabet below,
fill in the blanks and reveal the secret words!

__ __ __ __ __ __ __ __

__ __ __ __ __ __ __ !

A	B	C	D	E	F	G	H	I

J	K	L	M	N	O	P	Q	R

S	T	U	V	W	X	Y	Z

WORD SEARCH

Find and circle the words in the puzzle below.

- OPTIMUS PRIME
- LEADER
- PROTECTOR
- AUTOBOT
- SEMI-TRUCK
- ION BLASTER

```
Q E T Y U I P W R Y A D L G F S
T Y V B X Z F H X B V M E F M L
O V K S J U A C B L N Q A T R K
A V Q W E C F R Q R G A D F O P
K O P T I M U S P R I M E X C Z
R E R T V L I F V C U R R D I N
T Y O K J S C T C V J F I E O D
C X T L F R Z X R L U H J V N B
R J E V M Q R Y I U P L J G B D
S O C G K N Z C B L C J G O L A
H P T P F D J B R U S K F H A Z
U V O X E W C V Q P I A L N S X
G X R X X M J S A U T O B O T J
X D S G U V W K R T S I U G E K
J R S I E I R T A Q L K G P R D
```

TRANSFORMERS
REVENGE OF THE FALLEN

Have a parent or caregiver cut out the puzzle pieces on the dotted lines. Mix up the pieces, and put the picture back together!

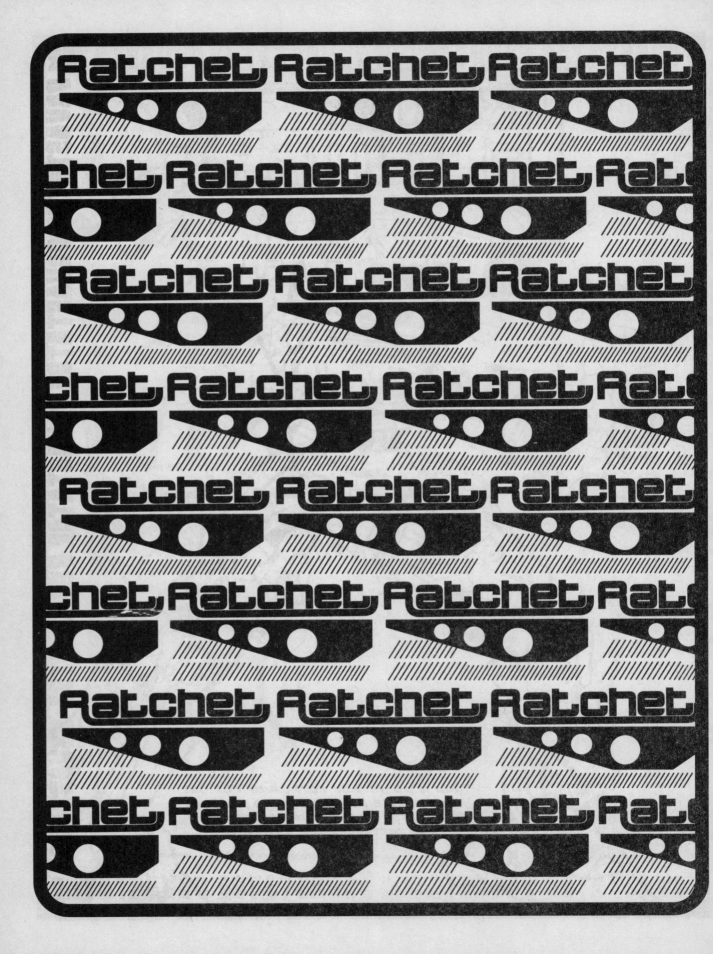

TIC-TAC-TOE

Use these spaces to challenge your family and friends.

Make a Match!

Only 2 characters below are exactly the same.
Can you find them?

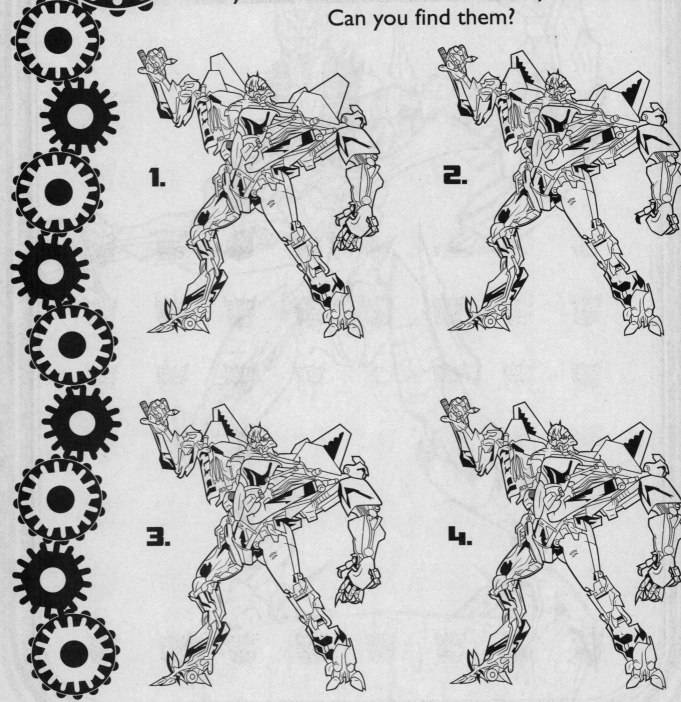

1.

2.

3.

4.

DECEPTICON SQUARES

Taking turns, connect a line from one  to another. Whoever makes the line that completes a box puts their initials inside that square. The person with the most squares at the end of the game wins!

OPTIMUS PRIME MAZE

Help OPTIMUS PRIME get through the maze to battle RAVAGE!

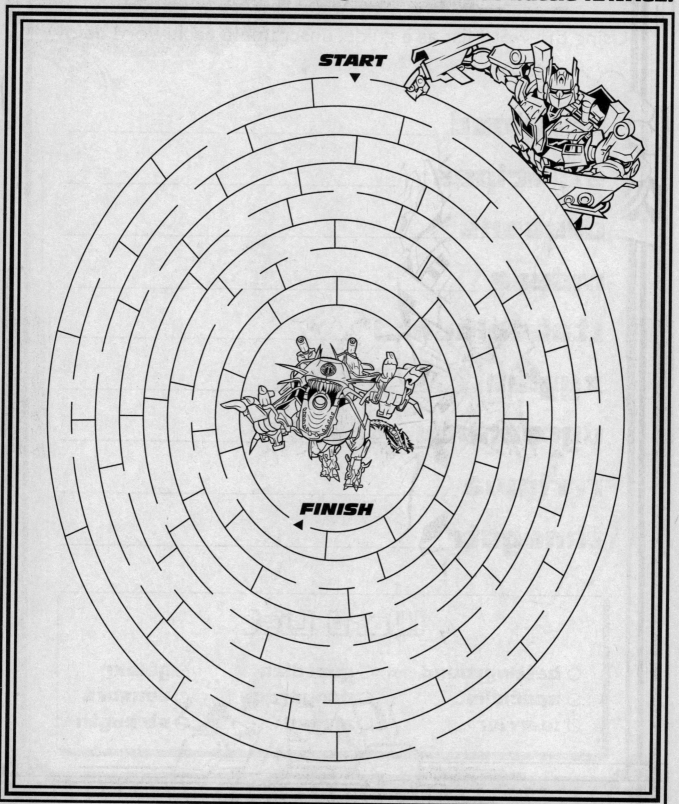

Word Scramble

Using the word list as a guide, unscramble each word below.

uarginad _____

stilacipes _____

orssens _____

mdera _____

ttabeglounrd _____

xyglaa _____

dgreansou _____

rrriowa _____

thnegstr _____

Word List

- battleground
- specialist
- warrior
- guardian
- dangerous
- armed
- galaxy
- sensors
- strength

WHICH IS WHICH?

Match each Transformer to its correct shadow.

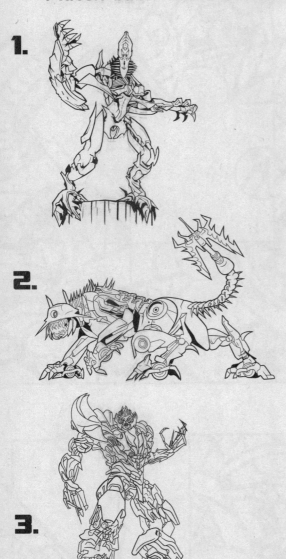

1.

2.

3.

Answer: 1. B, 2. A, 3. C

Which Piece is MISSING?

Only one of the puzzle pieces below will fit. Can you find the missing piece and complete the puzzle?

A.

B.

C.

Answer: C.

WHICH PIECE IS MISSING?

Only one of the puzzle pieces below will fit. Can you find the missing piece and complete the picture of Optimus Prime?

1.

2.

WHO is WHO?

Match each Robot to his name.

A.

B.

C.

D.

E.

F.

G.

H.

BUMBLEBEE

DEVASTATOR

Sideswipe

the Fallen

IRONHIDE

MEGATRON

STARSCREAM

OPTIMUS PRIME

TIC-TAC-TOE

Use these spaces to challenge your family and friends.

RATCHET

TRANSFORMERS
REVENGE OF THE FALLEN

WHICH RAVAGE IS

DIFFERENT?

One RAVAGE below is an imposter.
Can you find the one that is different
from the others?

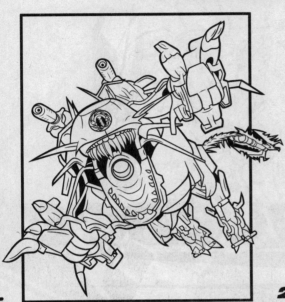

1.

2.

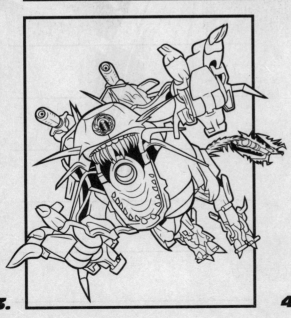

3.

4.

HOW MANY WORDS

can you make out of

BUMBLEBEE

_____   _____

_____   _____

_____   _____

_____   _____

_____   _____

_____   _____

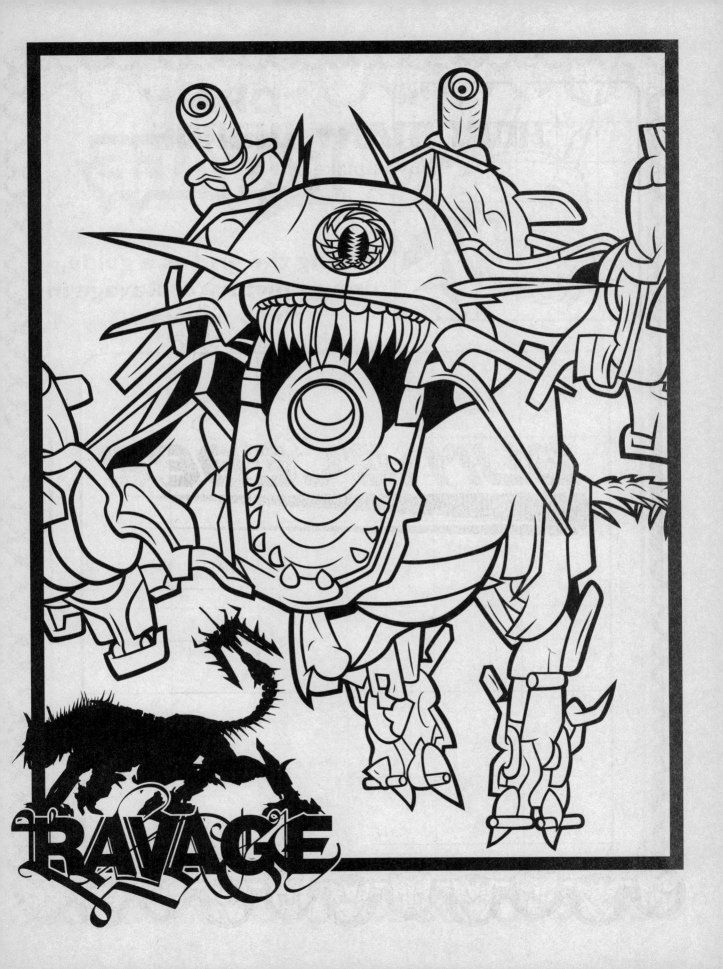

DRAW
RAVAGE

Using the grid as a guide, draw a picture of Ravage in the box below.

Follow the Path

Using the letters in order from the word

MEGATRON

follow the correct path to find your way through the maze!

START ▼

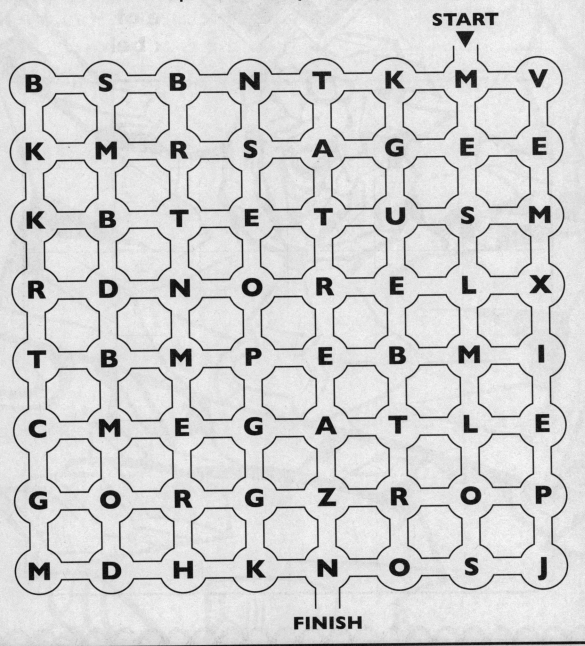

FINISH

OPTIMUS PRIME MAZE

Optimus Prime needs your help!
Can you find your way to the center of the maze?

Start

WORD SEARCH

Find and circle the words in the puzzle below.

- ○ MEGATRON
- ○ RAVAGE
- ○ STARSCREAM
- ○ RATCHET
- ○ SIDESWIPE
- ○ DEVASTATOR

```
Q E T Y U R P W R Y A O L G F S
T Y V B X Z A S X B V M E F M L
D V K S J U R T B L N O A T R K
A V Q W E C F A C R R E W T L P
K O P J O S U R P H O M C K C Z
R E R T V L I S I D E S W I P E
T Y O K J S C C R Y V T I E G O
C X L L F R Z R R J A H J V N B
R J E S D E C E S E S L J G B O
S T C G K N Z A B L T J G O L A
H P T P F O J M E G A T R O N Z
U V O X E W C V Q P T A L N S A
B I E K T L O F N Y O U G I Q C
H O H W E A P T R H R A V A G E
S J B K E O O M P W A E L B Q I
```

WHICH DEVASTATOR IS

DIFFERENT?

One DEVASTATOR below is an imposter. Can you find the one that is different from the others?

1.

2.

3.

4.

IRONHIDE SQUARES

Taking turns, connect a line from one 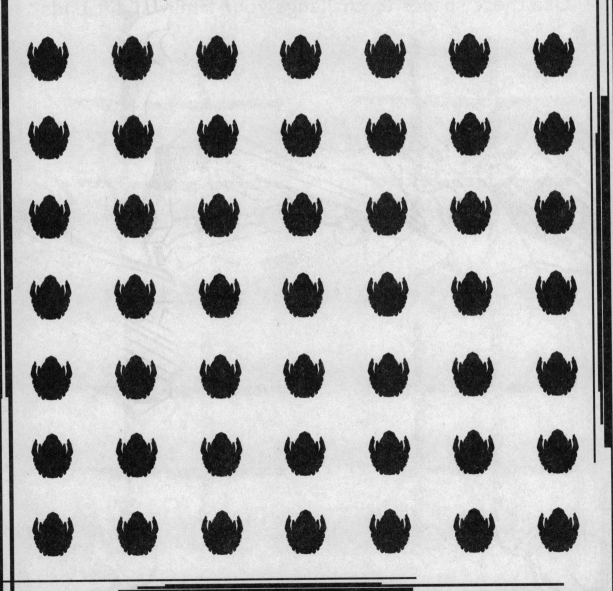 to another. Whoever makes the line that completes a box puts their initials inside that square. The person with the most squares at the end of the game wins!

TIC-TAC-TOE

Use these spaces to challenge your family and friends.

BUMBLEBEE

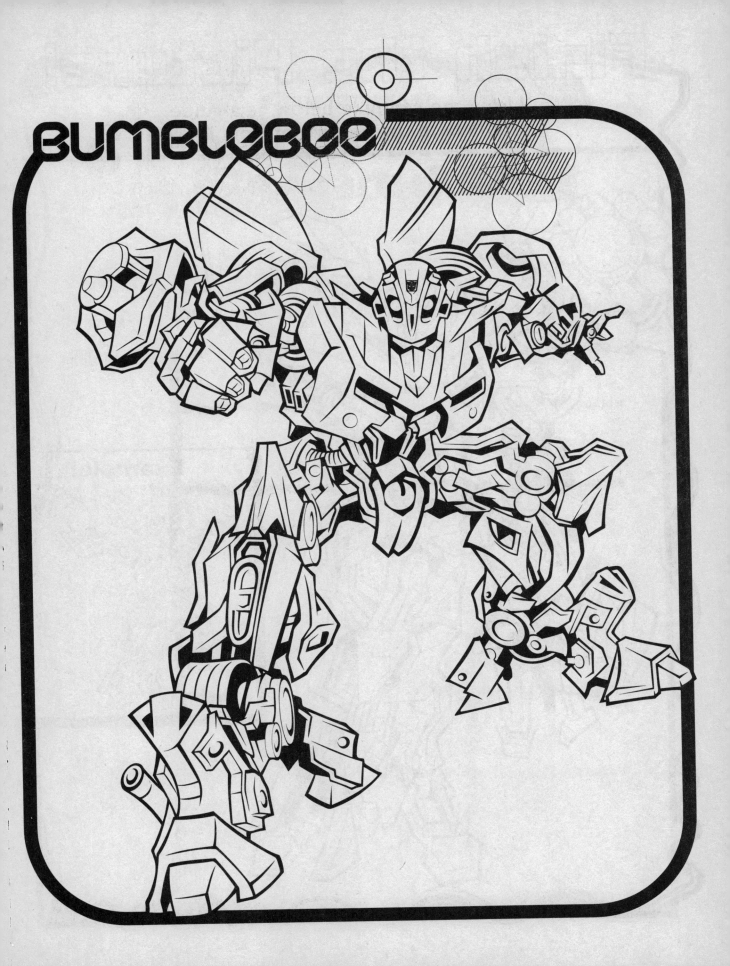

Finish the Picture!

Using the example below as a guide,
complete the picture of Ironhide.

Example:

TRANSFORMERS
REVENGE OF THE FALLEN

PUZZLE

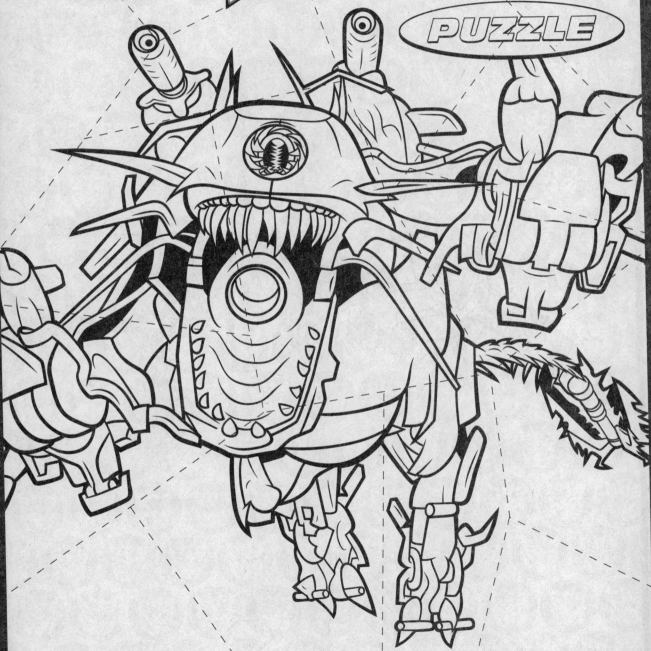

Have a parent or caregiver cut out the puzzle pieces on the dotted lines. Mix up the pieces, and put the picture back together!

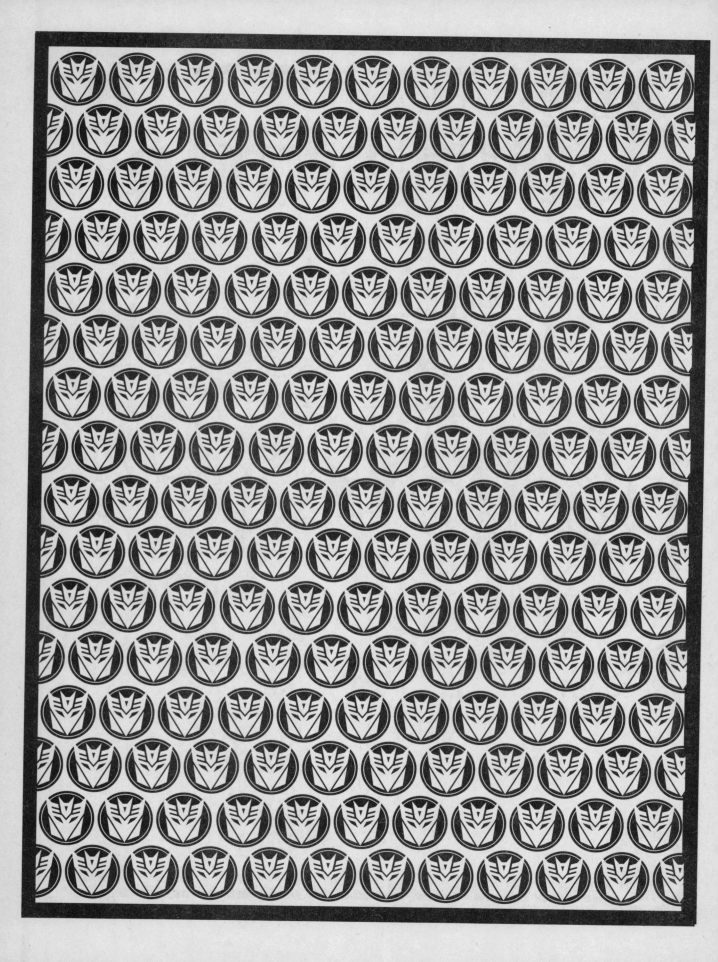

Cross out the word **SIDESWIPE** every time you see it in the box. When you reach a letter that does not belong, write it in the circles below to reveal the secret message.

SIDESWIPEASIDESWIPERS
IDESWIPEMSIDESWIPESID
ESWIPESIDESWIPEESIDES
WIPEDSIDESWIPEASIDESW
IPENSIDESWIPEDSIDESWI
PEDSIDESWIPEASIDESWIP
ENSIDESWIPEGSIDESWIPE
ESIDESWIPERSIDESWIPEO
SIDESWIPESIDESWIPEUSI
DESWIPESIDESWIPES

○ ○ ○ ○ ○   ○ ○ ○

○ ○ ○ ○ ○ ○ ○ ○ ○ ○

Make a Match!

Only 2 characters below are exactly the same.
Can you find them?

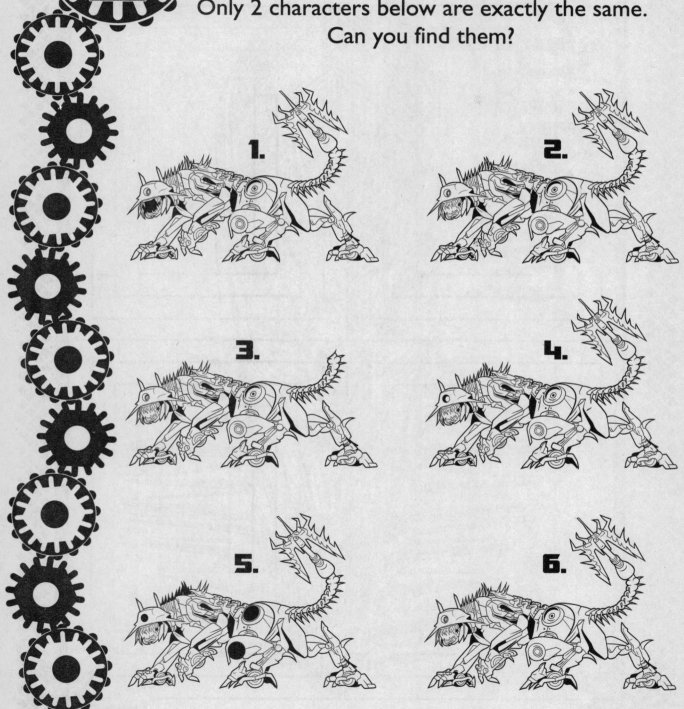

There is only one way out! See if you can find your way through the maze without running into The Fallen.

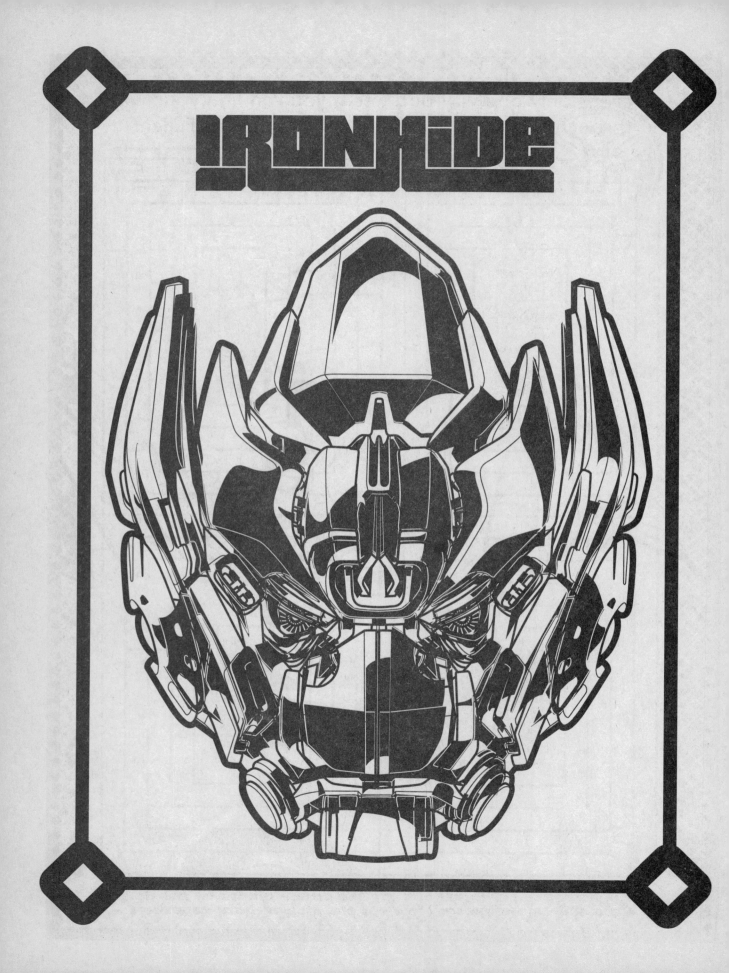

Have a parent or caregiver cut out the puzzle pieces on the dotted lines. Mix up the pieces, and put the picture back together!

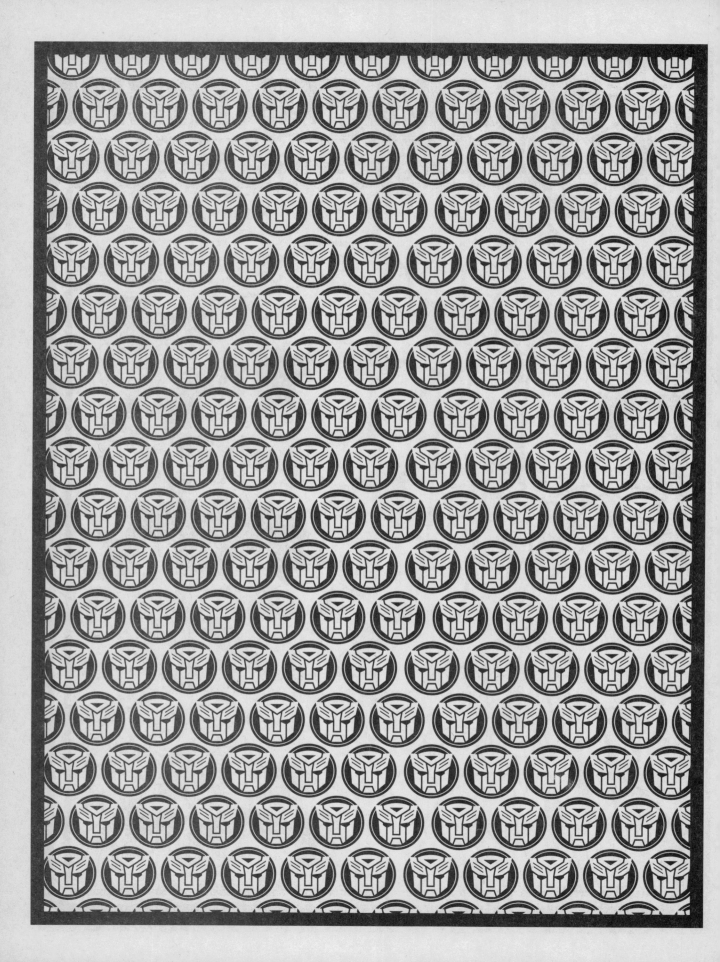

TRANSFORMERS
REVENGE OF THE FALLEN

WHICH IS WHICH?

Match each Decepticon to its correct shadow.

1.

 **A**

2.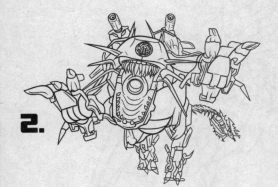

 **B**

3.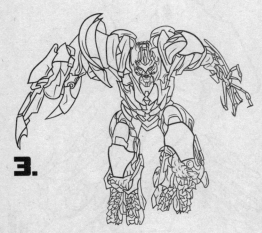

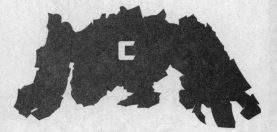 **C**

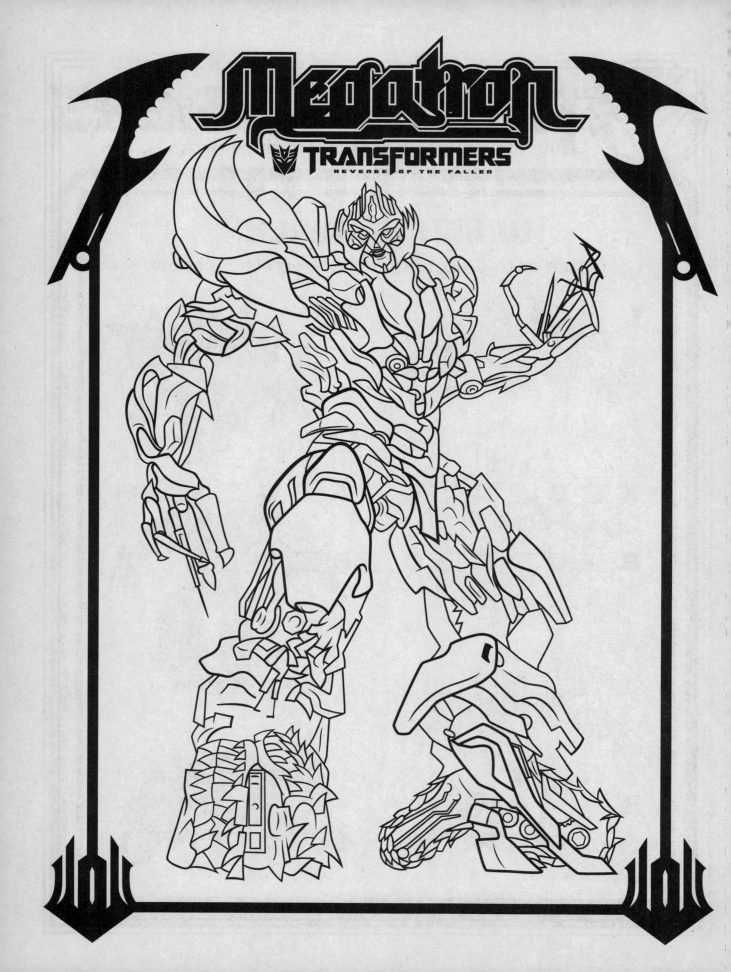

Follow the Path

Using the letters in order from the words

THE FALLEN

follow the correct path to find your way through the maze!

START ▼

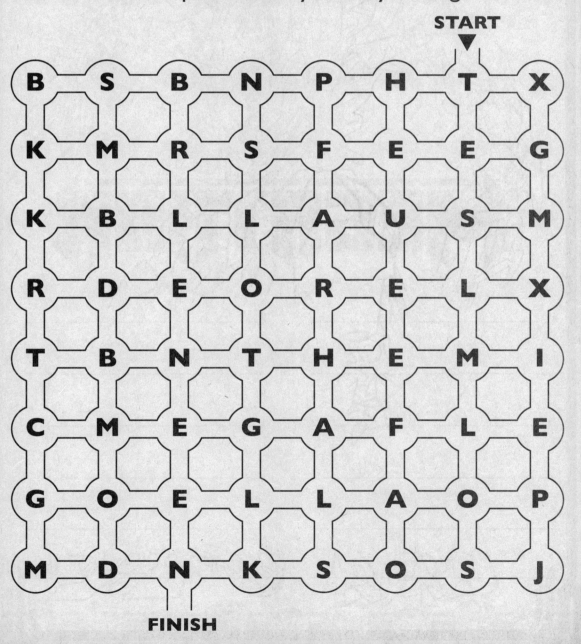

B	S	B	N	P	H	T	X
K	M	R	S	F	E	E	G
K	B	L	L	A	U	S	M
R	D	E	O	R	E	L	X
T	B	N	T	H	E	M	I
C	M	E	G	A	F	L	E
G	O	E	L	L	A	O	P
M	D	N	K	S	O	S	J

FINISH

HOW MANY WORDS
can you make out of

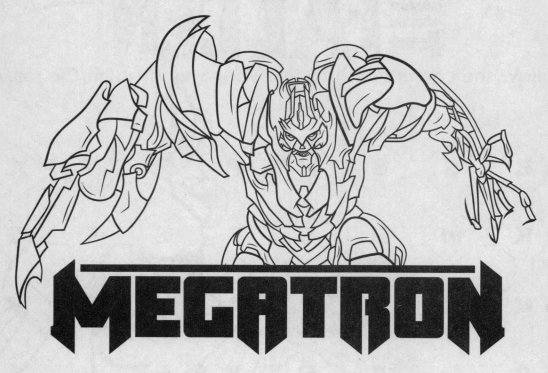

MEGATRON

_____   _____

_____   _____

_____   _____

_____   _____

_____   _____

WORD SEARCH

Find and circle the words in the puzzle below.

- ALLSPARK
- DANGEROUS
- EARTHQUAKE
- GALAXY
- WARRIOR
- COMMANDER

```
P W R X T Q Q Q E W Z C K F E R
S X U A W X Z R D W U L D E L M
C U J R I T O S G A L A X Y Q J
Z U P Q D B E J B R O D X G F K
Q C O M M A N D E R P K M K F D
Z X V C J F G T W I E K J G M C
B V B N S T H Y R D E U I U O P
N T S A D A N G E R O U S H G D
Q M F U F G L O M P G H E R I O
F C B A H G T L K B C A J H P W
J K F G L E K G S N B F Y D M N
S A V X I X C N G P F W K J L A
V B E M T K Q T N S A D B N U Y
R G H K L A Y T P O B R E J S E
T S B E E A R T H Q U A K E P N
```

DRAW
STAR
SCREAM

Using the grid as a guide, draw a picture of Starscream in the box below.

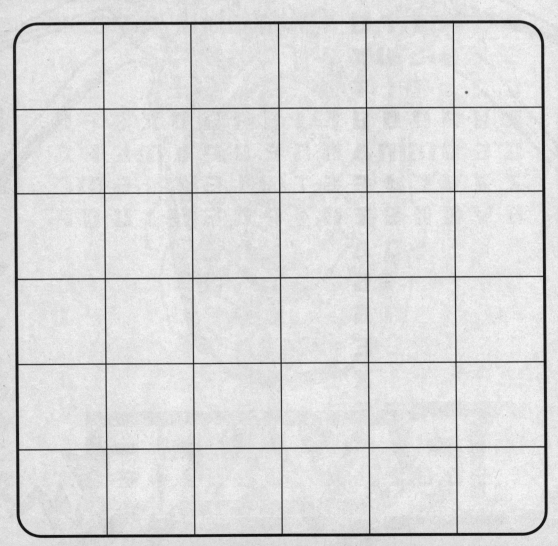

Finish the Picture!

Using the example below as a guide,
complete the picture of Sideswipe.

Example:

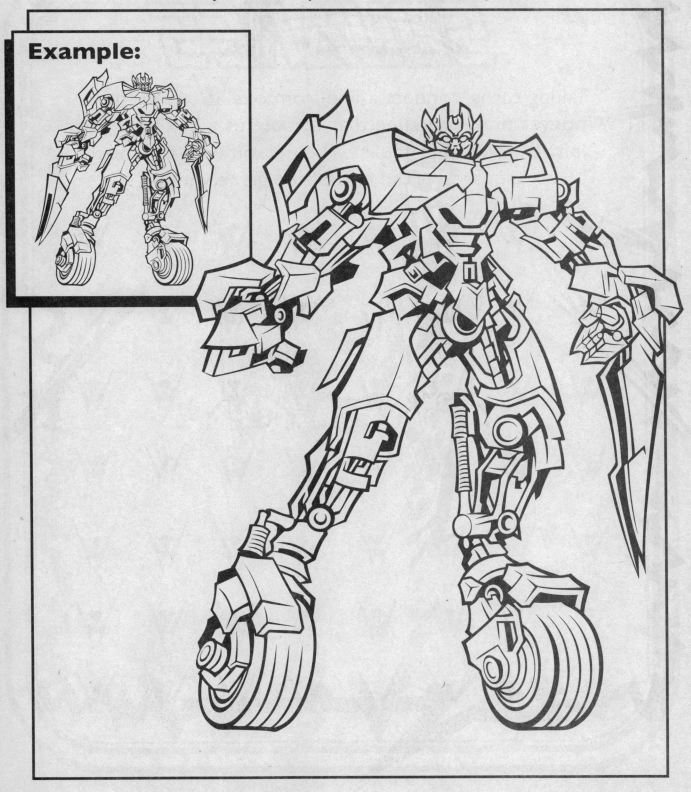

SIDESWIPE SQUARES

Taking turns, connect a line from one  to another. Whoever makes the line that completes a box puts their initials inside that square. The person with the most squares at the end of the game wins!

WHICH PIECE IS MISSING?

Only one of the puzzle pieces below will fit. Can you find the missing piece and complete the picture of Sideswipe?

1.

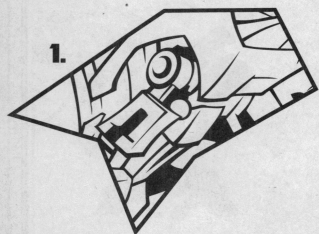

2.

WHICH IS WHICH?

Match each Transformer to its correct shadow.

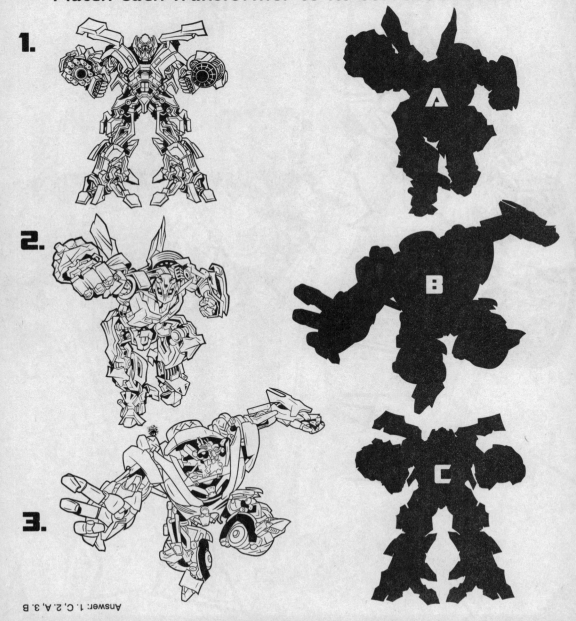

1.

2.

3.

A

B

C

Answer: 1. C, 2. A, 3. B

BUMBLEBEE

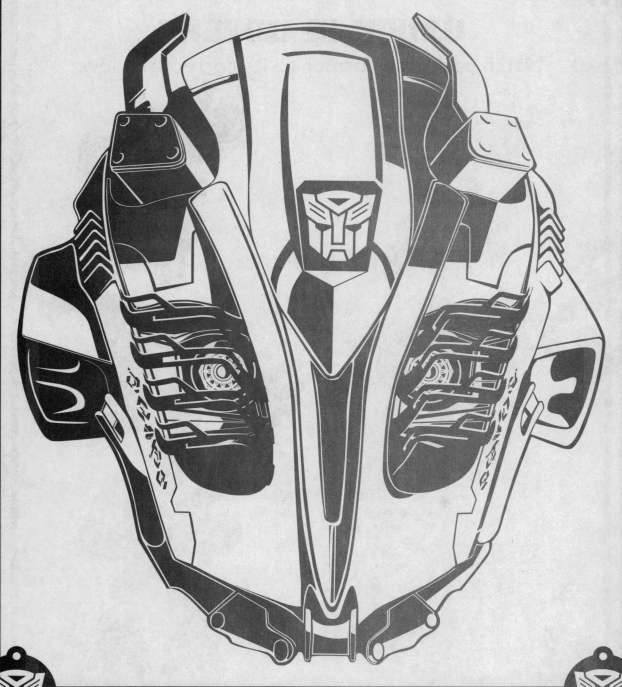

Make a Match!

Only 2 characters below are exactly the same.
Can you find them?

1.

2.

3.

4.